WHOEVER DROWNED HERE

WHOEVER DROWNED HERE

NEW AND SELECTED POEMS

ぷ

Max Sessner

TRANSLATED BY
FRANCESCA BELL

🐓 Red Hen Press | *Pasadena, CA*

Poems from *Warum gerade heute* and *Küchen und Zügen* © Literaturverlag Droschl, Graz-Wien 2005.

Poems from *Das Wasser von gestern: Gedichte*. Copyright © 2019 by Max Sessner. Used and translated by permission of edition AZUR.

Book design by Mark E. Cull

Library of Congress Cataloging-in-Publication Data

Names: Sessner, Max, 1959– author. | Bell, Francesca, 1967– translator.
Title: Whoever drowned here: new and selected poems / Max Sessner;
  translated by Francesca Bell.
Description: First edition. | Pasadena, CA: Red Hen Press, [2023]
Identifiers: LCCN 2023016195 (print) | LCCN 2023016196 (ebook) | ISBN
  9781636281384 (hardcover) | ISBN 9781636281391 (ebook)
Classification: LCC PT2721.E77 W48 2023 (print) | LCC PT2721.E77 (ebook)
  | DDC 831/.92—dc23/eng/20230407
LC record available at https://lccn.loc.gov/2023016195
LC ebook record available at https://lccn.loc.gov/2023016196

The National Endowment for the Arts, the Los Angeles County Arts Commission, the Ahmanson Foundation, the Dwight Stuart Youth Fund, the Max Factor Family Foundation, the Pasadena Tournament of Roses Foundation, the Pasadena Arts & Culture Commission and the City of Pasadena Cultural Affairs Division, the City of Los Angeles Department of Cultural Affairs, the Audrey & Sydney Irmas Charitable Foundation, the Meta & George Rosenberg Foundation, the Albert and Elaine Borchard Foundation, the Adams Family Foundation, Amazon Literary Partnership, the Sam Francis Foundation, and the Mara W. Breech Foundation partially support Red Hen Press.

First Edition
Published by Red Hen Press
www.redhen.org

ACKNOWLEDGMENTS

Grateful acknowledgment is made to the editors of the journals where the following translations (sometimes in earlier versions) first appeared:

Arc: "A Tidy Guest," "Ghosts," "Our Fathers," "Song," "Table;" *B O D Y*: "A Landscape," "Birthdays," "Dolls," "In the Café," "Shadows," "While Leaving the Café;" *Five Points*: "Man with Dog;" *Lyrikline*: "Days," "Half-Finished Drawing," "She's Always Dancing," "Summer with Lassie," "The Gold Tooth;" *Massachusetts Review*: "The Last Day of Winter;" *Meat for Tea*: "An Elderly Couple," "Die Mittagsstunde," "Summer Evening in Arles"; *Mid-American Review*: "At Night," "Ghost," "In the Circle of the Family," "Luise," "Shaving Man," "The Girl with the Heineken Bottle," "The Trains at Night," "Train Whistle at Night," "The Silence;" *New England Review*: "Ascension to Heaven," "Some Guests," "Visit"; *On the Seawall*: "Poppy," "Rembetika for Cavafy," "Sundays," "The Hülsenbeck Children;" *Rattle*: "August Evening," "It Is;" *River Styx*: "Apparitions," "Portrait of an Old Woman Sitting on a Park Bench," "Swimming;" *Waxwing*: "A Dry Cleaner's" (as "A Dry Cleaners").

Max wishes to thank the editors of *B O D Y*, who first opened the doors of the English literary world to his work, and Red Hen Press, for believing in this book enough to turn it from a possibility into a reality. Above all, he thanks Francesca, for this marvelous translation and for all the effort and care she took with his poems.

Francesca wishes to thank Noor Nader Al Abed, for helping her to find the courage to translate poems, and Angelika Quirk, for her keen editorial eye. Most of all, she thanks Max Sessner, for writing these beautiful poems and for trusting her to escort them over the border into English.

for Daniela
—Max

for Annelies, Angelika, and Annegret,
who taught me most of what I know of German
and much of what I know of life
—Francesca

Contents

II

from *Why Especially Today*

III

from *The Water of Yesterday*

IV

New

Translator's Note

Ultimately, the one true principle he stood for was the mystery
inherent in objects, in the world, that mystery which belongs to
everyone and to no one.
　　—Marcel Paquet, *René Magritte: Thought Rendered Visible*

I first stumbled upon the poems of Max Sessner in 2018, in the prestigious Austrian literary journal *manuskripte*. I'd been translating poetry for a few years and was looking for a poet with an extensive body of work that I could set out into, breathless and hopeful and enthralled, the way an old-time explorer entered a new territory. I found the eleven poems featured in *manuskripte* entrancing and wonderfully odd, and I immediately ordered Sessner's two most recent books and wrote to ask his permission to begin translating his work.

I was surprised to learn that Max Sessner's poetry, though widely celebrated in the German-speaking world, had not yet appeared in English. Sessner's work is profoundly relevant to our time, grappling as it does with the painful predicament of modern humans: how to live with the estrangement inherent to a life spent in thrall to objects. The poems also lend themselves gracefully to translation. They are accessible though complex; deeply, tenderly human; finely and carefully wrought; and possessed of a voice that is unique and compelling.

Max Sessner was born in 1959, in Fürth, in what was then West Germany, into a home without a single book of poetry. He did not study writing in college; he did not go to college. If contemporary German literature were a city, Sessner would live on its outskirts, near the river, on his own terms. He does not frequent literary conferences, or festivals, or the academic world, and does not concern himself with the latest poetic styles or trends. He has long lived with his wife in Augsburg—not geographically distant from his birthplace but feeling a world away—where he has worked as a bookseller, for the Augsburg Public Library, and for the Department of Public Health.

When constructing his poems, Sessner eschews nearly all punctuation. I have found a question mark here or there, but only when one was deemed urgently necessary. Just the first word of each poem and, following the German rule, all nouns are capitalized. Lines are broken with great care but in unexpected places and always in a manner that allows as many meanings as possible to emerge. In translating, I have necessarily rearranged words to reflect the differences between English and German sentence structure but have worked to retain the dream-like, surprising ambiguity that Sessner's strategies achieve.

To enter the poems of Max Sessner is to enter a world so fantastical it could only be *this* world, this real, surreal place that overflows with the strange magic of the ordinary. Sessner's landscape is the landscape of fairy tales and hauntings, where each human life is a house inhabited, in a very literal sense, by inanimate objects and the whispery, spectral wanderings of our losses and regrets. Pieces of furniture laugh at the old man who stumbles among them in his home at night. A dreamer knocks "timidly / at the window of wakefulness." A man's reflected face stays up later than he does and looks out, sighing, from its vantage point, the mirror. Time is at once an accordion in Sessner's hands— stretched to its full, wailing length and then compressed, singing—and a dwelling of many rooms, all inhabited simultaneously. We live life, these poems say, and life lives us, all at once, the past and the present entangled like lovers' limbs. Max Sessner's poetry is a poetry of comfort and loneliness, of sorrow but also of the sweet, lingering hilarity that lilts through even our darkest days.

WHOEVER DROWNED HERE

Some hop on board, some wave farewell
Or weep at the beauty of the crossing bell
But we all shall live again

—"We Shall Live Again,"
The Felice Brothers

I

from *Kitchens and Trains*

The Hülsenbeck Children

—Philipp Otto Runge, 1805/06

The Hülsenbeck children
those were three children who
loved each other one often ran across
them in the garden the youngest sitting
in a tiny wagon pulled
by the siblings but
how was that did they ever
reach the house the table with the
supper father and mother the
sunflowers stood high
that summer we searched in
ponds in graves they remained
vanished in the house the parents
withered so it goes

At Night

Nothing seems right here
the wind whips branches against the window as if
it wants to chase away the house a ghost house
all along with tchotchkes silence and old
parents the furnishings tell each other jokes about
the old man whose hair grows thinner and thinner
a sky without stars four times he pisses
at night four times down the stairs and four
times up into the petrified bed his wheezing
breath is like a fox out of a fairytale
by the Brothers Grimm that snuffles through
the dark rooms in order to reach the end
of the fairytale from where it's no longer
far up to the trees

Rembetika for Cavafy

On your beautiful young men who
sometimes visited your grave
dust falls today they are naked
as you like it best and
pluck at themselves bored
evening light seeps through the
shutters their lovers are coming
from the harbor antique sailors who
love on the floorboards and in the
room a scent of diesel and
ocean what is your hand doing old
poet just now their kisses
pain you in this dirty
city their goodbyes their
muscles the motor coaches drone
like an empty poem

A Dry Cleaner's

for burial shrouds (or was it the
smocks of small business owners)
I saw in Fulda at night
they hung tidy in rank
and file a train of first graders
going across a crosswalk
the empty sleeves
moved gently as if
hands wanted to get out
when we lay long since in
hotel beds fingers touched
each other traded stolen
caresses and finally
also rings in the light of
the shop window it probably
looked like nothing
but what do we really know

The Last Day of Winter

They are smoking outside the
students of the dance school
right next to the cemetery
it is the last day of
winter they are young and
over-perfumed the trees
lean towards the
evening and the air is a
novel without beginning
and end two of the girls
giggle their fingers fly to
the face of a boy who
bursts out brightly laughing
there's something crystalline to it
then they're called in again a
waltz someone claps
their hands it sounds like
a slap in the face but no one
runs crying back into the
street where we wait for
the bus as if for a miracle

Song

My father was a rolling
stone he rolled down
the street so long that nothing
more was left of him then
one swept the remnants under a
table where one sadly sat
and guzzled booze from big
glasses till morning

Our Fathers

Our fathers die and grow back in
the front yards of our houses and look at
us they wear boots with heavy soles
nights they march with them through our
dreams bring us with you when you wake
they whisper and we thrash in our sleep
and start to sweat our wives
notice none of this they nod and
pass us the jam at breakfast
on the way to work later how should one
say it a sound of steps in us
a slamming of doors within someone goes someone
comes turns on the lights and our eyes glow

It Is

Sunday and the bells
toll to services one last
look in the mirror and
the pastor climbs into the pulpit
I want a new car
Father in heaven but something always
goes amiss and so we find
instead in the evening an
injured blackbird in the garden you
bloody your dress as you
carry it carefully into the house it doesn't
bother you maybe you say
we'll remember this day years from now
or we'll dream of it
my love your hair by the way
is going gray bit by bit and the bird will
likely not survive the night

A Tidy Guest

for Jonathan Carroll

Death is already trying on
your clothes and walks
around the apartment in them while
you sleep in your best suit
he mugs before the mirror
he is well-bred
and tidy furthermore
he loves sweets and sinks his
teeth into your chocolate supply
a bad habit
as he admits but for it
you receive a few days
gratis and he even waters
your miserable
houseplants before he
goes and you awaken a
barely discernible smell
of moist earth hanging in
your laundry and your pants
pinch suddenly with each step
as you go down the stairs
what a peculiar
morning you think and you don't
feel comfortable in your own
skin that actually doesn't
belong to you anymore and like a
borrowed coat doesn't quite
go with your shoes

August Evening

and chlorine scent on my shirt from
the swimming pool the aunts
are there smiling slipping me
small change and what do you
want to be someday they
ask the spirit I say of a
boy who drowned last
year while swimming
his bicycle still stood in winter
in front of the pool oh they sigh
and one scuttles to the bathroom
no one budges until
finally there's a flush

Poppy

Between the remains of the burnt down
factory building that finally belongs to
the wind and the adolescent taggers
here where my parents slaved
yearslong from shift to shift and the
beauty of my mother sank into a
metal locker here grows with shy
condescension as one knows it
from young girls and mirrored in
bottle shards a stalk of red poppy

Apparitions

Today I saw you on the
street as an old woman
you walked past me and
I who died before you saw myself
mirrored in your glasses
as a young man you looked
right through me with a
gaze as if from an open
window out of which you will
soon jump down onto this
street in front of a moving car
whose driver looks like me

Man with Dog

When she left him he
bought himself a dog the
coat brown and white a
pretty animal I saw them
often in the fields behind
the freeway he quiet the
dog playful and yappy
always bringing pieces of wood
that he had to throw in
a high arc the
people say he must have
moved away one day
and no one realized it
but I've a notion that
one time instead of a stick
the dog brought the
whole forest and then
into it they both
disappeared

Sundays

On Sundays the game
with the ball in the dark
corner of the yard where
rusted-out tools
lay and my father once
stepped on a nail I found
the bloody shoe under a
lawn chair strange
ship with a pain-sail there
it had run aground
with its language
that no one understood

Train Whistle at Night

Strange year many
in town died
and it is true that
an old man led
his sick brother to
the railroad embankment
and helped him lie down on
the tracks pain has
colored the woods black
for always

Swimming

Now it is still on the little
lake mid-August the shadows
have deserted the trees and
have first wandered to the shore and
then dived under to
the bottom it makes the water
light if one approaches from the village
the lake in the distance looks like
an eye that stares into the
sky beginning in August it's the
melancholy that drives me to go
swimming after work
until far into the dusk I
lie on my back and let myself
be carried see on land the beacons
of the cigarettes whoever drowned here
always years after came back

The Silence

Today it is so
quiet in the house as if
the children had died
and you and I
grieved silently in the
kitchen their
grown-cold food

II

from *Why Especially Today*

Ascension to Heaven

This crow this morning
and the question of how
it looks inside it is there
room enough for me any
chair I can sit on
books periodicals I

won't fly without my dog
assuming a
storm should discomfort us are

safety precautions
met or will we
be utterly
at its mercy
I don't have any baggage

only a pocketknife to get
out of my skin
faster in case we someday

need a roof over our
heads because nothing
really belongs to us have you heard
now leave your
little stick dog and come

The Girl with the Heineken Bottle

—William Eggleston, 1975

He's asking himself where you are so
where are you girl this
morning he was still putting
your laundry in the closet now
he doesn't know what to do with his
hands smokes goes outside
in case perhaps you'll finally come
the late bus stops you don't
get out and his hands
grasp in the clouds a little
finger strokes the moon and
night scent so peculiar barely
lets him keep breathing and you in
your beautiful dress shimmering
green like a small
summer pond with circling
dragonflies stand unmoved in
the smoke of the cigarettes and look
at yourself for a moment
in the glass of the already half-
emptied bottle that green
as your dress seems to
float in your hand
you two could be sisters

Childhood Room

This is how I imagine the
afterlife my old
childhood room the view
out the window goes
down to the garden a few
apple trees flowerbeds
and the well-tended
lawn at night the roses
open their doors there
I don't want to know more I
count the books in the
single bookcase twelve they
stand close together
barely any dust on their
spines whoever cleans
here feeds this
room with time the bed
too small for me groans as
I sit down on the
mattress it sounds like
lovely to see you but
is it really you
I don't know only
how does one explain to a
bed that one thing leads
to another when one
least expects it

Once

Once we are thrown
back from the light
to the dark side
of the playing field after
a clean throw
the net remains
motionless
no quiver nothing only
one rippling little
dust cloud that
rises from the ground
and blows over

Some Guests

My toenail this morning black
and sore because of a pinching
shoe reminds me don't ask why of
the guest at a funeral who is still
sitting before a half-full beer when everyone
has already gone no one could remember
him a distant relative from
a different city unfashionable the dark
suit and doesn't he actually have brilliantine
in his hair now he's humming a hymn and
taps along with his knuckles on the
table let's see he thinks and stands up who
makes it home faster little soul you or I

Visit

My poem doesn't want to be
a poem anymore it has
set off disguised
as one of us
it is unrecognizable
even I would walk
right by it a small mortal
thing that no one notices

it is going to look
for work and start
a family a house on the edge
of town why not perhaps
I will pay it a visit
sometime after many years
friendships should be
cultivated like gardens it

said once and I
will repeat the sentence
and possibly the poem
will remember a perfect
host who leads me
through the rooms with tiny
steps even faster than the
second hand of my watch

The New Car

The whole family stands before the
new car that gleams in the
driveway happy sheet of metal
that mirrors the close-together faces
a bouquet of blue balloons
that suddenly soars I don't
know what I should say but
it really is beautiful honk the
horn someone says and Father
honks that brings Mother to blooming
her perfume rises in our noses
a neighbor flings a window open
I could sing like a bird

Ball Games

What is time the
gap between words
the never-said
the bathwater from which
someone climbs and with
wet feet runs through
the apartment once
I threw a ball onto
the roof and the ball
didn't fall back again
years later after a
storm it lay suddenly
in the garden what
happened we asked
ourselves and at night
you dreamed of a house
without doors the only
furniture a table and
a chair where someone
had already sat
for eons and looked
motionless out the window
that was the worst he
was old you said old old
old with a skin one
could see through
but there was

nothing no bones
or sinews nothing at all
but you saw us
didn't you

The Year That Wasn't

I always carry the year that wasn't
around with me sometimes in quiet
hours I set it before me on the
table and try to live in it I
don't often succeed but on good days

I build a house on one of the hills
in the middle of greenery and I am happy
everything smells all the way into dreams
of fresh paint from the living room
I watch the tomatoes ripening

and now you come into play you
call me outside you've placed
the old kitchen table under the trees
wobbly as my heart says
the poet in me who becomes less

and less soon just a granule that
wanders through my body
prods here and there until I sit
at the doctor's again with dry mouth
and damp hands but now

everything is still okay we uncork the
bottle and give the evening a
bit of magic and laughter and finally
the poet is also quiet at this time
he doesn't trust language anymore

Shaving Man

All these years I haven't
forgotten him
the man who
shaved every evening
at the kitchen table
under the kitchen light
in an undershirt the chin
covered with foam in
the mirror before him his
face a face
that wished him a good
night and stayed
awake a little bit longer
than he who went to bed
earlier and earlier
that looked around on the table
with the oilcloth
and listened out into the
quiet apartment
then gradually faded
the nose first
somewhat slower
the ears the eyes
as if they were flying
back into the darkness
and at last
with a small
sigh the mouth

In the Café

for Joe

This dog
how he looks at me
as if we must have known each other
I pay and
we chat a little longer
once we were
like brothers he says
and lays his paw
on my knee that was
long ago and if you
don't remember anymore
I can understand
but I still see
everything before me
as if it were yesterday
the old hick town
and us forever young
but in the end
I—mouth still full
of morning air—totalled
the car and myself
your grief was great
and your tears genuine
many years have
vanished and today
what a surprise
we run into

each other again
do you have children
are you a happy man
tell me fast before we
lose each other
again someone is already
pulling on my leash
and what about you
shouldn't you already
be home
by now

Luise

When she spoke with me
the last time she was still alive
it was in Vienna and I slept
like the snow on the rooftops
and nothing could wake me
she stood there before me and held
as usual her knitting in
her hands and knitted while we
talked a sweater of
dark wool it was impossibly
one for me it seemed enormous
to me if you followed one of the
sleeves you would definitely
get lost a shudder ran through
me already I knocked timidly
at the window of wakefulness and
simultaneous with me the snow
opened its eyes shimmered
in the early light as if it
had also been dreaming I stayed in bed
and so I fell asleep once
more but Luise didn't show
herself there was no news
of her no slip of paper with her
tiny script

Victor Emil Janssen

after a self-portrait, 1829

When he had peered the room
empty what remained there the
chair he sat on a piece
of paper on his knees the pencil
in the pants pocket so he
began to draw himself his
face as if a second a third
lay beneath and so on
the hands small and slightly
hunched the back the head
nearly detached from the neck there
I am again now he said quietly
astonished he looked around the
table with the wildflower bouquet
in the corner the unmade bed
everything as always in its
place the windows finally brought
the wind the evening
street knocked at the house from the
furniture the pain rose into his
bones and back again

Ghost

Fifty years ago my father started
his car in order to be here
today he already didn't smoke anymore
back then so he drank coffee and ate what
ended up under his tires on the endless
streets he saw himself in the rearview mirror
getting older his beard went gray then white
he gave the gas stations the names of his
unborn children in summer he sang
until his tears came at some point
his clothes disintegrated into thin air
and he froze until today we all wait
in suspense stand at the fence and look
down the street Mother baked
a cake in celebration of this day
we breathe slowly now he's coming his
car shoots up the driveway the
clanking of sheet metal a cloud of
dust that settles on Mother's roses
then silence we hear a beard rustle
but it is nothing and again only nothing

In the Circle of the Family

Grandpa turned eighty
and everyone came
every adult is
a short rhyming poem

on this day
the children scurry like
commas through the house
small mysterious anthology

I cannot read you
without getting tired
my eyes always close
after the foreword

never will I discover
why I'm here
already there where the bookmark is tucked
there's no one who knows me

Things

If we don't love things
they haunt us one
day they fall out of their world

into ours and a smell
clings to them that we don't
know the stuffed dog

lost a long time ago one-eyed
and with only three legs left sat
one morning next to our

bed he spoke to you with my
voice how alien we suddenly were
to each other the morning sun cast

my head as a shadow on the
wall and it resembled a coffee cup
that you loved and that I threw

to the floor once in a rage
broken into a hundred shards
it took to the road

on that day I saw them everywhere
returned they took possession
of us dolls naked

and without heads waved
to us and toy clocks displayed
toy time I rode away

from you on a bicycle
that was eaten away
half by rust and half by sadness

III

from *The Water of Yesterday*

Ghosts

Because we had recently discussed
ghosts and what sort we perhaps
would be should it ever come to that
I thought it over for a long time today
I cannot imagine being one of

the evil kind that comes up
to beds with a face of ash
and spreads rumors in people's
dreams desolate stuff that

causes them to awaken clueless and
listening to their inner voices as if in a
dark wood such a ghost never
but one who drops by casually
a few bottles of beer in the bag

and already makes itself at home
in the kitchen long before midnight
approaching the matter completely relaxed
and from whom nothing more remains

than a slight beer vapor in the
rooms when he disappears around
morning a ghost like that wouldn't be
the worst even if he also slammed
the door so violently shut

She's Always Dancing

for Christian Futscher

The girl who always wants to dance
is I suspect in the skin
of my old neighbor lady from the house
across the street three times a day summer

as in winter she leaves the house goes
with graceful little steps her feet
in house slippers to her compact car
parked in the courtyard entrance circles

it repeatedly finally stands still
and stares out into the street as if
into something dark applause is whispering
in the darkness and a murmur hangs in

the air it is a little bit macabre
but also a little bit beautiful when
you stand by chance at the window you
involuntarily smooth down your hair

Portrait of an Old Woman
Sitting on a Park Bench

In passing one sees behind her
face that's still beautiful a second
younger one then a third a fourth and
last somewhat smaller the face of a
girl and if a lover long since lost
kissed her now passing as I did
by chance her first face
would open up and all the others
would fall between her feet like
coins from a purse into the gravel

Table

Today I am the table at which
you sit yesterday I was something
else but I can do tables
the best of all furniture
I like them the most but

only the wooden ones which
remind me of old dogs that
watch over our sleep
loyal and philosophical my
minor talent fails at

chairs too complicated I've
tried never have I managed
a flawless exemplar tables
on the other hand I can do
from a standing start and you

just propped your elbows on
me laid your head in your
hands and are looking
down at me I don't feel so very
comfortable with it your glance has

after all something reckless and
I feel a pricking in the wood
as you abruptly pull out the
drawer it is completely empty
forgive me this small vanity

Shadows

Now the shadows wander into
the house they are like grandmothers
who look around one more time
before they leave us in

passing they arrange
the flowers in the vases ascend
the stairs and are
shadows again settle

on beds and furniture and also
they take up residence in us a
fragrance of violets wafts from
our hair and the rustling of

their clothes is not intended for
other ears how thin they
have become fallen from
language they swiftly wither

While Leaving the Café

The girl takes the
umbrella or
does the umbrella take
the girl
lead her out into the wet
evening and
touch her softly on the hand
seeing them from a distance
one thinks of lovers
the wind plays with the
girl's hair
and the umbrella is speechless
with joy

Summer with Lassie

At the end everything was always
good again one stood in a
kitchen and laughed someone drank
a glass of milk the dog looked

at me and I looked out the
window it smelled of lilacs
and urine Grandma the alien
lingered a little in front of the

television before she pulled the plug
with a sigh everyone disappeared
the laughing family and the
laughing dog the whole summer

I lied through my teeth and yet
it is true that I survived
adventures once I fell from the moon
and someone threw me back

The Trains at Night

Do you hear the trains at night my old
dog can hear them we are of differing
opinion about departure and arrival

to a certain extent it's because of the
summer night a soft glove
that falls upon our eyes when we

try to sleep five empty
fingers that comfort us that reach
for nothing no glass no medicine

A Landscape

In the not-too-distant future
I will be old I have
seen it coming yes a train
approaching you stand
on the railway embankment throw

your arms in the air as if you want
to wave to a friendly
face behind the windows
but everything goes much too fast
the train is gone before you

know it and you
stay behind in a dull
place it is completely
still no bird that takes flight
not a waft of air as

if you're standing on a
rug that begins to roll
up from its edges
you're tempted
to hop or to hide yourself

behind a bush
but there isn't one so
you stand still and think
a little about God
it is like before only different

The Gold Tooth

Do you know happiness is an
idiot it never really knows
where it should be seated when it
finally sits it often stands right
up again walks through the
streets as a no longer entirely

young man in threadbare
clothing one can imagine
that he sleeps in building
entryways but there is this
magical moment this
flash of a gold tooth

in the evening light when he
settles down after all and
tugs someone on the sleeve
perhaps no idiot at all just
someone who is too shy
to loudly clap his hands

Dolls

Time has passed the toys have
grown tired the dolls of the
girl look altogether cleverer than
the girl herself what a
shock when they learned that the
girl was gone now married and

in a different city one of the dolls
consequently lost all her hair another
the right arm the dearest of all
was never found no one searched
very long for her either just
to imagine she had gone after the girl

is lovely but what if it's true and
tattered and dirty she lay
one evening in front of the door just the
thought of it keeps me from sleeping
and with my hands forming a funnel
I call something into the quiet house

Birthdays

Mother was busy the whole day
with her roses she
loved roses above all else no face
could compete with that a
handful of snow was my

birthday present there take it
she said but say nothing of it to Father
Father had run away with
another woman so what
could I have said to him that the

snow melted as it lay on my
palm and became
a small lake on whose
shore a city arose in
which one more time I grew up

Days

Where have the days gone do they still exist
somewhere the wedding day all the
birthdays there cannot be a cemetery
for days and also who would
maintain the graves there no one

could ever finish planting flowers
on each one but I have heard
that they stand as small houses
in a suburb close together
the streets poorly lit like in

an old American film someone
who ended up there by chance said
the doors were only slightly ajar and
all houses looked the same from the outside
so that one easily lost one's bearings

also there were no shops
nowhere one could chat a little
so he drove on and on at a
walking pace letting the radio play until
his gas gradually ran low

he would have liked to experience his
tenth birthday once more of all the days
he could best remember that one
but where should he search so
he turned around thought of that day

forty-five years ago of his mother
who possibly stood there still
and for all eternity had to repeat
the one sentence over and over
Now finally do blow the candles out

A Blackbird

for Ulrich Ostermeir

The garden is very quiet in the
evenings there are garrulous gardens
this one though is quiet like
the pocket comb that someone has
forgotten on a bench he
who has forgotten it runs his

fingers through his hair now
and wishes in this moment
nothing more fervently
than to be a blackbird it is
because of the song that
rises in him dark and tender

while he orders a
glass of red wine in the bar he taps
the beat on the tabletop with his
hand he sits like that for a
while and hums to himself
then he begins to drink

An Elderly Couple

after Jan Gossaert, 1520

Fine dust has fallen on their faces
has settled in the wrinkles of the
forehead in the corners of the mouth
where a smile only seldom reaches
now and if it does a bit of dust
rises and hovers in front of their lips
a little before it comes to rest again
mostly they're silent each to themselves
they are quiet little rooms in the

same house light wanders unspeakably
slowly across the furniture sometimes
it lingers touches an object
longer picks it out of its shadow
and puts it quickly back
there are days they meet in the
hallway and don't recognize
each other they greet then like
strangers he carries his old duffel bag

under his arm and she done up
as if for a lover displays the prettiest
of her dresses together they go forth
one hears their steps from room
to room their quiet conversation only
a whisper by the end he has
opened the bag she has first thrown
the dress over a chair and then
laid it carefully folded in his bag

Half-Finished Drawing

Dying never but becoming one
with the slipcover of the sofa offers
a possibility of gentle
disappearance with a smile
and my hands in my pockets I am
barely visible anymore only those

who love me still recognize my
features in the pattern of the cloth there are
evenings one sees me somewhat
more distinctly it may be due to the weather
I don't know then you sit next
to me your hand on my knee and

barely legible a tiny script appears
on the back of your hand
you move your lips silently
as you try to read your heart
knocks strongly it knocks outside of
you somewhere in this room

Die Mittagsstunde

—*Edgar Ende, 1946*

I have never seen the midday like this
that an angel could arrive
standing in a boat with a
long oar and would silently stand before

our balcony we would be confused and
bewildered leaving the vacuum cleaner
singing as if this would change anything
and would nevertheless step out in order

to assure ourselves he would offer me a friendly
handshake pull me over tenderly oh
what a drag now I have to float
with him through the blue eternally I know

you would wave to me in farewell
for someone always stays behind does
the laundry makes the bed feeds the cat forgets
her name becomes light as paper

Summer Evening in Arles

—Van Gogh, 1888

I'm always just Sessner and you
forever van Gogh the way the ears
of wheat glow tiny mirrors before which
insects make themselves beautiful on
a path two people walk I
think they are lovers it is

one evening among many the light
perhaps somewhat softer than usual
in some people there's a
noise as if someone were throwing
coins onto the table and it sounds
like a laugh scornful and silvery

and it never returns like the
smoke that rises from the chimneys
or words of joy and happiness
whispered in the dark on
this day years ago you breathed
in and today I breathe out

IV

New

Flowers

for Francesca

A sandy path up to the
nursery and the quiet scent
of the plants someone is binding
flowers into a bouquet it's the

one for my mother that
I'm to pick up I often awaken
exactly at this point and
feel in the dark for my

glasses as if I'd be able
to see the ending although I do
know how it will finish no
closing credits no music just a

boy with a bouquet of flowers
who runs through my sleep
as if running through a labyrinth
always following the smell of the
flowers as the only clue

How We Dream

And all the strands of lights above
the square and your face in the paper lantern
memory is nothing and yet the
always recurring dream of
an apartment where we live
and the back part of which we never
enter although it's also furnished
just dustier everything with tracks
of little animals do you hear my
heart beating as I talk about it
even though you are somewhere else at
this moment paying for your
purchases or speaking with someone
who long ago oh well but you already know
this gap between here and there
a soft movement of the stars
precisely now and imprecisely also

Encounter

We talked about all sorts of things
about poets we once knew
about how expensive everything had become
and that the cat of an acquaintance
disappeared for days there was
no more proof of its existence only

in her dreams it often appeared
but always as if it belonged to someone
else a cold comfort we thought
and the story of a friend occurred
to you too complicated to
tell so it went back and forth

this standing-next-to-each-other was puzzling
random and fruitless until I
heard myself say at the end yes
see you later and we went our ways and
I know that I thought for whatever reason:
the last ride in the carriage belongs to you

News

There's barely news of the poems
anymore sometimes they send
someone to pick me up and
bring me to a location someone I don't
know a car stops in front of my
house and waits with a running motor
often for hours and hours I can see from the

window how it gleams in the morning
sun it is tempting but listen
I'm not going out there I'd rather clean
the house from top to bottom and
get lost in it years elapse
before anyone finds me hair matted
and barely skin and bones

I am no pleasure to look at and
still this is better than to end up who
knows where the barrel of a gun to
the back of my head and blindfolded
losing the ground under my feet
to live in fear perhaps for all time
they'll get me they always get you

One Day

Everything comes back to haunt us
one day the boy you beat
up a long time ago
stands before you in the street car
he is like you now around

sixty his hair thin like
yours generally he looks
like you moves like
you as he approaches you
walks past gets off

at the next stop
that was it you turn
after him and note
the stop and tomorrow
you'll have forgotten it

Stories

In every life there is a hook
on which nothing special hangs

Grandfather's hat he wore
to his wedding and no
longer at his funeral

or a pair of roller skates
rusty the wheels barely
movable anymore I can
remember the sound
that they made on the
summery asphalt

all the things that point back
at something else on and on

at the end stands a bawling
child all that clutter ahead a giant
mountain he doesn't know where to start
the path is so far and all the
hooks that must be mounted

and such a stupid story
and that's how it always was told

Pennsylvania Coal Town

—Edward Hopper, 1947

The man is tired he just fixed the sink
in his kitchen after work
it's cool in the house the living room
already lies in the shade

he hears the ticking of the wall clock
the television is off the woman
in town at the doctor at the hairdresser
he couldn't say

tick tock says the clock
he fetches the rake from the cellar goes
out to the grass he is no philosopher
what he knows he knows period

he's wearing a dark vest a light
shirt and he is bald off his head
reflects the sunlight that someone
seems to pour out the light

is pure like his shirt the grass under
his feet glows he looks up
he is the sum of it all without
realizing it he is who he is

Photo, the Forties

So it was
your dance under the apple tree
and we ask ourselves how
does she even do that
without touching even one
branch
the photo is already somewhat
yellowed torn on the edges
for days I had it on my
desk
and didn't figure it out now
it occurs to me it is
the tree that holds you
immerses you in its
shadows where
your body flows back to
only your face remains in
the light defiant
eyes wide open it doesn't
want it simply doesn't
want to disappear
forever in front of us

Wanderlust

Don't mistake your soul
for one of the shirts that
are draped over chairs in the wan
light of the morning it should sing
like a bird but it remains
mute has no answer
to your questions only after

breakfast is it entirely
yours like a shadow it goes
through your days reminds you
of trivialities and of what
you will one day forget until you
forget yourself then it is
free makes its approach jumps

dressed in one of your loveliest
shirts into the next blue sky
from there it isn't much farther
and a desire to hike comes over
it it is very light
finally it brings not one gram
too many to the scales at the border

Waves

We stood on the shore and threw
stones into the water and you were first
to discover the village that looked
like ours only it lay at the bottom

of the lake but the street was
recognizable on which our houses
stood up above a light wind dragged
across the water and small waves

lapped at our feet an
illusion perhaps but then
below a light went on and
I can't say which one of us

would most have liked to jump
and submerge leaving clothes
behind on shore as proof
that it's possible to live down there

Biographical Notes

Max Sessner was born in 1959 in Fürth, Germany. He has long lived with his wife in Augsburg and has held a wide variety of jobs, working as a bookseller, for the Department of Public Health, and currently for the Augsburg Public Library. Sessner is the author of eight books of poetry including, most recently, *Das Wasser von Gestern* (*The Water of Yesterday*), published by edition AZUR in 2019, and *Küchen und Züge* (*Kitchens and Trains*) and *Warum Gerade Heute* (*Why Especially Today*), both from Literaturverlag Droschl. Among other honors, he was awarded the 2019 Rotahorn Literary Prize.

Francesca Bell is a poet and translator and is the current poet laureate of Marin County. Her debut collection, *Bright Stain* (Red Hen Press, 2019), was a finalist for the Washington State Book Award and the Julie Suk Award. She is also the author of *What Small Sound* (Red Hen Press, 2023), and her work appears widely in literary journals. Bell grew up in Washington and Idaho and did not complete middle school, high school, or college. She lives with her family in Novato, CA.